DEC 2020

D1117326

LET'S HATCH CHICKS!

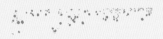

Inspiring | Educating | Creating | Entertaining

Brimming with creative inspiration, how-to projects, and useful information to enrich your everyday life, Quarto Knows is a favorite destination for those pursuing their interests and passions. Visit our site and dig deeper with our books into your area of interest: Quarto Creates, Quarto Cooks, Quarto Homes, Quarto Lives, Quarto Drives, Quarto Explores, Quarto Gifts, or Quarto Kids.

First published in 2018 by Young Voyageur Press, an imprint of The Quarto Group, 100 Cummings Center, Suite 265-D, Beverly, MA 01915, USA. T (978) 282-9590 F (978) 283-2742 QuartoKnows.com

Young Voyageur Press titles are also available at discount for retail, wholesale, promotional, and bulk purchase. For details, contact the Special Sales Manager by email at specialsales@quarto.com or by mail at The Quarto Group, Attn: Special Sales Manager, 100 Cummings Center, Suite 265-D, Beverly, MA 01915, USA.

10 9 8 7 6 5 4 3

ISBN: 978-0-7603-5785-9

Cataloging-in-Publication Data is on file with the Library of Congress.

Acquiring Editor: Thom O'Hearn
Project Manager: Alyssa Lochner
Art Director: Laura Drew
Cover Designer: Mighty Media
Layout: Mighty Media

Printed in China

LET'S HATCH CHICKS!

EXPLORE THE WONDERFUL WORLD OF CHICKENS AND EGGS

BY LISA STEELE

ILLUSTRATED BY
PERRY TAYLOR

young
voyageur

CONTENTS

MEET VIOLET!

Violet is a gray chicken. She lives on a small farm in the country with her **flock**. Her yard has lots of grass and trees. That's where the chickens play. Sometimes Violet's human family shares treats with the chickens. They like lettuce, strawberries, and seeds. Violet runs around and eats as many seeds as she can! The chickens lay eggs for the family to eat.

TAKING A BATH

The chickens have a nice **coop** to sleep in at night. There's a **dust bath** nearby. Chickens don't take baths with water. They use dirt to keep their **feathers** clean! Can you spot the chicken in the dust bath?

VIOLET FINDS A NESTING BOX

One spring day, Violet left her friends in the yard. She had decided it was time to become a mother **hen**! She headed back to the coop. Violet peeked into each **nesting box**. Then she chose one she liked best. It was quiet and dark. It had lots of straw **bedding** to keep her eggs safe. It even had curtains across the front.

FEELING BROODY

The family noticed Violet wasn't outside playing with her friends and they were worried. Was she sick? No, Violet was **broody**!

Some broody chickens seem angry. They puff up and make growling noises if you get too close to their nests! Don't worry, she isn't mad at you. She is just protecting her eggs. They will soon become her **chicks**.

ROOSTERS AND EGGS

Most eggs in a chicken coop are just like the ones you eat. They will never **hatch** into baby chicks. But if a **rooster fertilizes** an egg while it is still inside the hen, that can change! When a hen lays a fertilized egg and keeps it warm for three weeks, an **embryo** grows inside the egg. The embryo is what will turn into a chick!

Eggs that are not fertilized cannot turn into chicks.

FEATHERING THE NEST

Violet began to lay eggs in her special nesting box. She still came out to eat her breakfast. But when her friends went out to play, Violet jumped back into the box.

Violet worked hard to make the nest perfect. She tugged at pieces of straw with her **beak**. She started pulling feathers out of her breast and placing them in the nest. The feathers made a soft bed for her chicks. Her bare skin helped keep the eggs warm.

MORE EGGS, PLEASE!

There was just one problem. Violet needed more eggs! She didn't want to sit on the eggs until her nest was full. The other chickens wanted to help. They laid their eggs in the nest. Kate, an Ameraucana, laid a blue egg. Annie, an Australorp, laid a pink egg. Abigail, an Olive Egger, laid a green egg. Soon, Violet's nest looked like an Easter basket!

HELP YOUR HEN

Once the nest was full, Violet spent more and more time on the eggs. She made the nest up just the way she wanted it. All the family could do was help. What can you do to help your hen?

- You can mark the eggs with a pencil. If any of the chickens sneak in and lay more eggs in the nest, you'll know, because those eggs won't have marks. Then you can take those eggs out, or all the eggs in the nest won't hatch at the same time.

- You can put a little dish of feed and a bowl of water close to the nest. She won't have to go far to get something to eat or drink.

- You can tuck a bit of lavender or chamomile into the straw. These herbs smell nice. They can keep your hen calm.

- Inside the house, make a special chicken calendar. Start marking off the days for three whole weeks. That way you'll know when the chicks are ready to hatch.

TURNING, TURNING

Inside the egg, a baby chick rests on the **yolk** and starts to float. If the egg doesn't get turned, the chick can get squashed between the yolk and the eggshell! Violet made sure to turn each egg over and over. She did it several times each day.

Violet also needed to keep all the eggs warm. She flattened her back and spread her wings out so all the eggs were covered. She made sure to move the eggs on the outside of the nest closer to the middle.

Violet even tossed pieces of straw onto her back. To keep the eggs safe, she was trying to hide herself in the nest so no one could see her!

Violet fussed over her eggs. She made happy clucking noises whenever the family went to check on her. She knew they were excited!

FUN FACT:

Baby chicks can hear a mother hen clucking to them while they're still in the **shell**!

NOW, WE WAIT...

Violet kept the eggs warm so chicks could grow inside them. She missed playing with her friends, but her eggs needed her. She was a little lonely. But soon she would have babies of her very own to keep her company! At night, the other chickens came back to the coop to sleep. Violet had plenty of company then. Everyone was inside, safe and sound on the **roost**.

HATCHING IN AN INCUBATOR

If you're hatching eggs at home, your family might use an **incubator**. If you have an incubator, you will need to be like the mother hen. You will need to turn the eggs! Here's how you do it:

1. First, you should wash your hands. There are germs on your hands you don't want to get on the eggs.

2. With your parents' help, open the incubator.

3. Use a pencil to mark one side of each egg with an X.

4. Turn the eggs carefully. Turn each egg so the mark is either on the bottom or the top, the opposite of the way it was before. Stop turning the eggs on day 18.

5. The last step is washing your hands again. There are germs on the eggs you don't want to leave on your hands.

What else can you do to help the chicks grow? After two weeks, if you cluck to the eggs, sometimes they will peep back at you! It's always fun to talk to your chicks.

WHAT'S GOING ON IN THERE?

As soon as the eggs are warm from morning through night, the chicks will begin to grow. Everything a chick needs comes from the egg:

- The egg yolk will be her food.

- The **albumen** helps to cushion the embryo while it grows. It shrinks as the embryo gets bigger.

- An **air sac** forms in the rounded end of each egg. That's what the chick will breathe until she is ready to hatch.

- Fresh air enters the egg through tiny holes in the shell called **pores**.

A chick needs three weeks to grow. Let's peek inside an egg and learn what is happening each day.

FIRST COME THE EYES AND WINGS

The eyes are one of the first things to form. By the fourth day, your chick's heart is beating and her wings have started to grow. Can you see the feathers on this chick's wing?

Day 1

- Head and brain start to grow
- Digestive system begins to form

Day 2

- Eyes begin to form
- Heart forms and starts beating

Day 3

- Wings and legs begin to form
- Tailbud forms

Day 4

- Tail appears
- Legs grow and toes form

BEAK, ELBOWS, KNEES, AND TOES

By the end of the first week, your chick will start to take shape inside the egg. Her legs and wings finish forming. She has a beak and even some toes! But she still has lots of growing to do.

Day 5

- Head grows bigger
- Sex is determined
- Elbows and knees develop

Day 6

- Beak and **egg tooth** form
- Ribs appear
- Embryo starts to move around

Day 7

- Beak and comb start to grow
- Neck forms
- Brain is developing
- Toes are visible

FUN FACT:

Chickens can see more colors than humans can! This helps them find bugs, seeds, and berries in the grass.

FUN FACT:

Most chickens have four toes on each foot.
But a few **breeds** have five toes on each foot!

CANDLING EGGS

Want to peek inside the egg? You can't crack it open. Try **candling** it instead! An egg candler lights up the egg so you can see what's happening in there. Try candling for the first time after one week. Try it again after two weeks. Just don't disturb the eggs after day 18.

WHAT YOU'LL SEE WHEN CANDLING

The first week you might see a spider shape. The "body" of the spider is the embryo. That will become the baby chick. The "legs" of the spider are blood vessels. They help the chick grow.

The second week you may find a big blobby shape. This means the chick is growing! Your chick will get bigger and bigger until it takes up nearly the whole egg.

If the inside of the egg is clear after two weeks, the chick did not develop. You can remove it from the incubator or from under the broody hen.

On day 18, you might see the chick move around. You might even hear it peep! Don't candle the egg after this day.

Note: Always remember to wash your hands before and after touching eggs.

THE BEAK IS FOR PEEPING

This week your baby chick will have ears. She will soon be able to hear the mother hen outside the egg. Her mouth can now open and close so she can "talk" to her mom when she hatches. Peep, peep! What will you say to your chicks?

Day 8

- **Down** starts to grow
- Ears and eyelids form

Day 9

- Mouth opens
- Claws develop on toes

Day 10

- First feathers appear
- **Nostrils** form
- Beak starts to harden

FUN FACT:

Chickens do more than peep, cluck, and crow. They can make up to thirty different sounds to talk to each other!

SHAKE THOSE TAIL FEATHERS

Now the chick is getting stronger. The eggshell gives her the calcium she needs for healthy bones. The chick will also finish growing most of her feathers.

Day 11

- Tail feathers grow
- Pads appear on bottoms of feet

Day 12

- Scales develop on legs and feet
- Hearing begins

Day 13

- Body is mostly covered with feathers

Day 14

- Head and ribs harden

THE FINAL STRETCH

We're getting close to the end! Your chick is almost done growing. She will start absorbing the egg yolk for nutrition. She will also move into "hatch position." This means she is almost ready to break out of the shell!

Day 15

- Scales on legs, claws, and beak harden
- Feathers finish growing

Day 16

- Albumen is nearly gone
- Chick starts to absorb the yolk for nourishment

Day 17

- Head turns towards the air space

FUN FACT:

A chicken's heart beats about three times as fast as yours.

Day 18

- Chick is almost done growing (there's no more space inside the egg!)

Day 19

- Beak rests against the egg's inner **membrane**
- Egg yolk is absorbed into the chick's body

Day 20

- Beak breaks through the membrane and makes an internal pip
- Lungs start to function

Day 21

- Oxygen is almost gone in the egg
- Egg tooth makes external pip through the shell
- Chick is breathing outside air

FUN FACT:

Chicks can see and walk as soon as they hatch. But they need their mom to keep them warm.

PIP, ZIP, PEEP!

For the last few days, Violet hardly left the nest. She sat on the eggs morning and night. The family could hear her clucking softly to her chicks.

The chicks were eager to get out! Some eggs were even starting to roll around. Finally, it was time for the chicks to hatch.

Each chick poked a small hole, called a **pip**, through its eggshell. The chicks rested for a few hours after they made the little hole. Hatching is hard work!

Once the chicks had rested up, each one used its legs to turn in a circle inside its shell. As it turns, the chick pecks around the shell until the whole top of the egg pops off. This is called the **zip**. Zipping the top of the egg can also take many hours.

Finally, the chicks used their legs to kick out of the shells. All of this can take a whole day or even two days, so the family was patient and waited. It was hard not to help, but they knew it was best to let the chicks do it themselves.

As each chick hatched, it rested for a while so its feathers dried and got fluffy. The family could hear peeping under Violet. They were excited to see the new babies, but knew they needed to wait.

SLEEPY TIME

Violet stayed close to the nest with her chicks. They spent a lot of time sleeping. Some even fell asleep standing up. Some chicks napped underneath Violet.

Violet and her chicks needed their own space for a few days. The other chickens were curious but they couldn't meet the chicks yet. Soon the chicks would be curious too, ready to get out and explore their new world.

BROODER BABIES

Sometimes a mother hen does not want to raise chicks. Or you might hatch eggs in an incubator with no mother hen. If this happens, your family will be the mother hen for your chicks!

You need to make them a home in a **brooder**. You can use a cardboard box, dog crate, or puppy playpen. You will need a **heat lamp**, a water dish, and a feed dish. You'll also want paper towels or dirt on the floor so it is soft and not slippery.

WHAT ELSE CAN YOU PUT IN THE BROODER?

- Add a few clumps of dirt and grass. Chicks love to nibble it and hunt for bugs.

- Add branches for the chicks to hop onto. They will learn to balance and roost.

- Hang a feather duster in the brooder. This looks like a mother hen and the chicks will love to snuggle under it.

FEEDING THE CHICKS

The family gave Violet a small plate of chick feed and a shallow dish of water. They put small stones in the water dish. That way the baby chicks couldn't fall in. Violet showed her chicks how to drink.

She showed them what to eat as well. She pecked at the little bits of chick feed. Baby chicks don't need to eat for the first two days after they hatch. But then they need to eat every day.

How do you feed your chicks?

- The chicks should have chick feed available all the time. They will get hungry at different times.

- You can sprinkle some raw oats or cornmeal on their food. This helps them stay healthy.

- Chicks like eating fresh herbs. Try giving them a little fresh parsley, oregano, or sage.

- Put out dirt or chick **grit**. Chicks use dirt like humans use teeth. It helps them digest their food.

HOLDING CHICKS

Chicks are like other kinds of babies. They are fragile and can get hurt. It is good to play with them, if you are careful. They will get to know you. Here are the steps for holding your chicks:

1   Sit on the floor and put a towel in your lap. Then have your parents place a chick on the towel. Put down your hand close to the chick. It will probably come right up to you.

2   Try putting your hand out on the ground, with your palm facing up. Let your chicks hop onto your hand. Sprinkle some chick feed onto your hand so they can peck at it.

3   Talk to your chicks so they get used to your voice.

4   Make sure an adult helps you pick up a baby chick. Scoop a chick up from underneath. Gently cradle its belly with *both hands* and place your thumbs over its back. If your hands are small, place one hand underneath and one on the chick's back.

Note: Children under the age of four or five might accidentally hurt chicks in their excitement. They might instead gently stroke the chicks while an adult holds them. And children of any age should never handle chicks without adult supervision.

Here are some tips for playing with your chicks:

• You should only play with your chicks for few minutes at a time. Chicks are babies and need lots of sleep.

• Chicks get cold quickly. If your chick starts peeping loudly, that means it's cold.

• Only play with one chick at a time. Chicks move fast. You don't want them to run and hide where you can't find them.

• Wash your hands after playtime so you don't get sick. Do not put your fingers in your eyes or mouth when you're playing with the chicks. Don't kiss the chicks.

CHICKS MEET THE CHICKENS

Soon Violet knew it was time to let the chicks meet the chickens. Sometimes a chicken can be mean to chicks. Most chickens are just curious. Violet stayed close to her chicks to make sure they did not get bullied. The family also watched to make sure the chicks were safe.

These chickens recognized the chicks from the coop. But if your chicks hatched in the house, you might have to keep them in a small cage outside for a while. The other chickens need to get used to them. Once everyone gets along, the chicks can join the chickens in the yard.

Note: Baby chicks that didn't hatch under a mother hen should never be left unsupervised with adult hens. They should be kept separate until they are about the same size as the larger chickens because they don't have a mother to protect them.

TIDBITTING IN THE YARD

Soon Violet roamed the yard with her chicks. She showed them how to look for bugs, berries, and weeds to eat. She taught them what was good to eat by **tidbitting**. If a chick tried to eat something bad, Violet pecked the chick on the head!

VIOLET THE TEACHER

Violet taught the chicks how to take dust baths. She showed them good places to hide from danger. She taught them how to hop up onto a small branch to take naps. She protected them and let them cuddle when they were cold.

GROWING UP

Violet kept teaching her chicks for five weeks. Then she left them on their own. She had taught her chicks well and they happily played outside, looking for bugs and good things to eat. They followed the others back to the coop when the sun went down. They were part of the flock!

The new chickens still had more growing to do. They look funny when they are teenagers! They have skinny necks and long legs. Their baby feathers fall out and they grow their "big girl" feathers.

FUN FACT:

Chickens should start laying eggs when they are four or five months old. Chickens can live to be more than ten years old, but usually will lay eggs for just a few years.

GOODBYE!

With the chicks all grown up, Violet returned to her old life. She played outside with the rest of the chickens and napped under the trees in the afternoon. She was happy to be back with her friends. The family wondered if she would want to hatch more chicks next spring. What do you think?

GLOSSARY

air sac: A round pocket of air inside the egg. It helps the chick breathe. Air enters the pocket through tiny holes in the eggshell.

albumen: The clear, runny inside of an egg. The albumen is also called the *egg white*. It acts like a pillow for a growing baby chick.

beak: A chicken's mouth. Beaks are hard and pointed to help the chicken eat and clean its feathers.

bedding: Material for the coop floor and nesting boxes. Chickens like soft bedding for laying eggs. Bedding can be straw, pine needles, or dried leaves.

breed: A group of animals that share traits. A breed of chickens looks and acts the same and lays the same color eggs. Ameraucana, Australorp, Lavender Orpington, and Olive Egger are all different breeds.

brooder: A baby chick's first home. It is like a nursery for newborn chicks.

broody: A broody chicken is one that wants to sit on eggs until they hatch into chicks.

candle/candling: Shining a light through an eggshell to see inside it.

chick: A baby chicken.

coop: A small shed or building that chickens live in. Chickens usually sleep in their coop.

down: The soft, fluffy covering over a baby chick's body. Chicks have down before they grow feathers.

dust bath: An area in the dirt where chickens like to wriggle around to clean their feathers.

egg tooth: The sharp point at the end of a baby chick's beak. Chicks use it to break a hole in the eggshell.

embryo: The cell inside a fertilized egg that will grow into a chick.

feathers: The covering on a chicken's body. Feathers help keep chickens warm.

fertilize: When a male's sperm combines with a female's egg. It is required for an egg to hatch into a chick.

flock: A group of chickens.

grit: Small stones or pebbles that chickens eat. Grit helps chickens digest food because they do not have teeth to crush the food.

hatch: The moment when a chick breaks out of the egg.

heat lamp: A special light that keeps baby chicks warm until they grow feathers.

hen: A female chicken over a year old. Hens can lay eggs.

incubator: An electric machine you can use to help you hatch eggs without a mother hen.

membrane: The thin lining inside an egg. The membrane separates the yolk and white from the shell.

nesting box: A box in a chicken coop filled with soft bedding. This is where a chicken lays her eggs.

nostril: The holes in a chicken's beak that let air in. Every chicken has two nostrils just like humans do in our noses.

pip: The hole a baby chick makes in the shell when it begins to hatch.

pores: Tiny holes in the eggshell. Pores let air into the egg.

roost: A pole or board inside the coop that chickens sleep on.

rooster: A male chicken that is over a year old. Roosters do not lay eggs.

shell: The hard exterior of an egg.

tidbitting: A clucking noise made by a mother hen. Chickens drop food in front of chicks and make this noise to teach them what to eat. Roosters can tidbit as well. Sometimes roosters dance when they tidbit!

yolk: The orange or yellow part of the egg that is packed with vitamins and nutrients.

zip: The circle a baby chick pecks in the eggshell when it's hatching.

ABOUT VIOLET AND LISA

Violet is a Lavender Orpington chicken. She lives on a farm in Maine with her family. She has raised two broods of chicks and is a proud aunt to many more. Violet loves to eat watermelon and scratch around looking for bugs.

Lisa Steele comes from a family of chicken-keepers. She is an author who writes about chickens and gardening. She likes to grow yummy vegetables for Violet and her sisters to eat. This is her first children's book.

Learn more about raising happy, healthy chickens at www.fresheggsdaily.com.

ABOUT PERRY

Perry Taylor is an illustrator who draws funny pictures of his life in rural southwest France. Perry lives with his wife in an old farmhouse. They have six chickens and a young rooster named Rusty. His website gallery is at www.perrytaylor.fr.